STEVE CAUTHEN

STEVE CAUTHEN

by Gloria D. Miklowitz

GROSSET & DUNLAP
A Filmways Company
Publishers. New York

PICTURE CREDITS:
Wide World Photos, pages vi, 2, 5, 8, 11, 15, 19, 22, 24, 32, 34, 35, 37, 40, 52, 54, 63, 70, 75, 76, 79, 82, 85, 87, 89;
Los Angeles Turf Club, Inc.-Santa Anita Park, pages 26, 28, 30, 57, 58, 67, 68, 73, 81;
California Breeders' Association, pages 43, 44, 47, 49, 50.

CONTENTS

I WANT TO BE A JOCKEY

"The horse is such a beautiful animal," says Steve Cauthen. "When you're on him, in control of him, moving with him as one, it is a beautiful feeling." Then, Steve adds softly, "The best is when you're almost getting him to know what you want to do."

Steve Cauthen is a jockey. He rides horses for a living. He travels from race track to race track, from New York to California, to ride. If he can bring his

horse in faster than the others he's racing against, he wins money for the horse's owner. In 1977, while he was only 17 years old, Steve rode many winning horses. His mounts won over $6 million. Steve earned nearly $600,000 for himself. The magazine *Sports Illustrated* named him "Sportsman of the Year." Three Eclipse Awards, racing's highest honors, were presented to him by the Thoroughbred Racing Association of the U.S.

Steve Cauthen was born on May 1, 1960. When he was only a year old, his mother Myra propped him up on a horse to pose for a picture. When he was two, he was already riding a pony.

It was natural for Steve to take to horses. His father, Ronald (Tex) Cauthen, grew up in Texas and worked around horses all his life. He earns his living as a blacksmith, shoeing horses at $27 each. Steve often went with his dad to the stables and tracks where he worked.

Steve holds the "Sportsman of the Year" Award. Wide World Photos

Myra, Steve's mother, grew up on a horse farm in Kentucky. It was only four miles from where they now live. Her father raised and owned horses. Myra not only rode, but became a trainer. She met Tex Cauthen at the track.

Steve was three when his parents took him to his first Kentucky Derby. The Derby is a very important race for three-year old horses. While his parents watched the races, Steve played in the grass and munched picnic goodies.

The Cauthens bought a 40-acre farm when Steve was five. It's in Walton, Kentucky, about 20 miles from Cincinnati. The town is small, only 1,600 people. Its biggest building is the high school.

The Cauthens keep broodmares (female horses for breeding) at their farm. In their living room are pictures of winning horses they have trained or ridden. Over the fireplace is a painting of a smith shoeing a horse. The shrill whistle of trains passing on the railroad track nearby can be heard from inside the house.

Steve loved helping with the

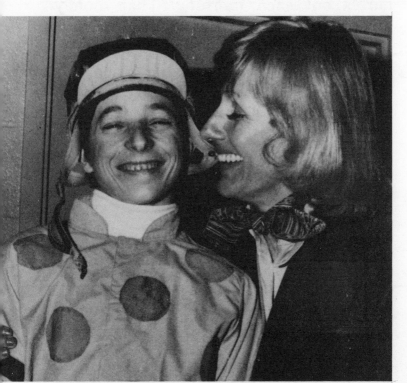

Steve with his mother. Wide World Photos

horses from the very start. He was paid $4 a week to clean the stalls and put the horses out each morning. That money went into the bank. He also got $2 spending money.

Once Steve watched a family friend training his best horse. It was a stallion named Slade. Slade was fast and strong. "Hey, Steve," the trainer kidded. "You want to ride this dude?"

"Yup," Steve said.

"Put the tack on him, boys. You sure you can do it Steve?"

"Yup."

The trainer wasn't sure if he should go through with the gag. But seven-year-old Steve mounted Slade. He walked him around the barn a few times.

"The first time they came around the corner, I could hardly believe it," the trainer said. "Old Slade was snorting. Baring his teeth. Throwing his head around something fierce. And Steve was laughing."

Steve liked most sports and was good at them when he was young. But his heart was in riding horses. He learned to groom and gallop at an early age. He showed ponies at the 4-H Club. He was breaking yearlings at nearby farms before he was even 12. "He could ride everything that moved. And even some things that didn't," his father says.

Then, when Steve was 12, he went to his father. "Dad," he said. "I think I want to be a jockey."

Steve walks through the barn area at Churchill Downs with his brother Kerry. Wide World Photos

CHAPTER TWO

THE "BUG" BOY

Mrs. Cauthen wasn't eager to see Steve become a jockey. She thought it was too dangerous. Often jockeys are thrown. They are sometimes badly hurt. "But Steve was determined," she says.

Steve's small size was part of the reason for his decision. Jockey's shouldn't weigh more than about 120 pounds, fully dressed, carrying their saddle. They also shouldn't be very tall.

Steve, at 12, was small for his age. He had been normal size and weight at birth. But for some reason he didn't grow

Steve in the starting gate at Belmont Park. Wide
World Photos

at a normal rate. He weighed 40 pounds when he was six. That showed only a 10 pound increase in five years.

"Race riding is something I can do in sports as a participator, not just a spectator," he said. "I liked all sports at one time—baseball, football, basketball, you name it. But being so small, I couldn't ever play them on an equal basis."

A jockey, then, was one thing he could be. A jockey was an athlete, just as a baseball player. But before deciding, Tex Cauthen took his son to several doctors. He wanted to find out if they could predict how much Steve might grow. "I was concerned that after all the training, he might grow six or seven inches and that would knock him out of business. It would be a terrible shock to him. A very hard thing to swallow after he had set his heart on becoming a jockey." But there was no doctor who could tell if or how much he would grow.

To help train, Tex told Steve to lift weights to increase his strength. He also suggested he do yoga exercises every morning.

"The routine is like a ballet dancer's," Tex says. "He keeps his legs and arms limber and supple so he can stretch back and hit a horse freely."

Steve began getting up at four in the morning to go to the barn. For two hours, while everyone else was asleep, he sat on a bale of hay. He pretended it was a horse. Using a jockey whip his parents bought him, he snapped the whip on the bale as if it were a horse coming down the stretch. "He cut up many a bale of $2.50 hay, learning," his mother says. But in time, he could flick that whip to within a hair of where he aimed it.

During summers for the next few years, he worked at local tracks. Other kids his age were going to movies or riding around in cars. But Steve was having the kind of fun he enjoyed. He mucked (cleaned) stalls, walked hots (horses hot from racing), and hung around the jockeys listening to their talk and watching what they did. He was especially interested in how they left the starting gate.

Little by little, he picked up the best habits of the best jockeys. His father helped, too. He began bringing home films from River Downs and Latonia race tracks. With a borrowed projector, Steve and his dad would spend evenings in Steve's room. They played the films again and again, backward and forward, seeing how moves were made. "There were maybe 80 or 90 races," Tex Cauthen says. "And we just about wore the film out. We talked about things that people don't talk about too much anymore. Wind resistance and balance. . . ."

When Steve races now, you can see the results of that study. He rides very low to cut the wind resistance. His back is so flat, it seems he could balance a cup of tea on it and not lose a drop. His face is buried in the horse's mane. Some jockeys have glanced his way during a race and thought he had fallen off.

Says Steve, "I give my father credit for everything I have learned. The

Riding low, so he's one with the horse, Steve won six races in one day, on two different days. Wide World Photos

basic things came from him: how to get a good seat and hands. Pace. How to switch the stick in one stride."

Steve couldn't enter racing as an apprentice until he was 16. He could hardly wait for his birthday. "I suppose I counted off the days on the calendar for a year," he recalls. On May 1, 1976, his sixteenth birthday, the waiting ended.

On May 12, Steve rode his first race. It was at Churchill Downs, in Kentucky. He was the youngest jockey riding. His horse was called King of Swat. Bettors gave him only one chance out of 136 to win. They were right. King of Swat came in last.

On May 17, at River Downs, Steve rode Red Pipe. The horse was owned by his mother and trained by an uncle. Red Pipe was given odds of 3 to 1 (meaning once chance out of three to win). Steve brought Red Pipe in first!

There's a ritual "bug boys" (apprentices) must go through after winning their first race. It's similar to young sailors crossing the international dateline at sea for the first time. "The older riders got me down in the jocks' room and covered me with shoe polish and a lot of other gook," Steve said. "Man, I looked hideous. But I relished the moment."

Steve brought home his fifth winner 10 days later. Until he rode that fifth winner, he had a triple "bug." That means a 10-pound weight allowance. An apprentice jockey is allowed to ride 10-pounds lighter than a regular jockey. Three stars, called "kisses" or "bugs," are put next to his name on the racing form. After five winners, the first "bug" is removed. The apprentice now competes with a seven-pound allowance, until he has won 35 races. After that, the apprentice (or bug boy) races with a five-pound allowance and one star next to his name. One year after his first win, he loses the weight allowance and becomes a regular jockey.

Of about 150 new apprentices each year, maybe five become successful jockeys. Another 20 can earn their living at racing. But the rest can't make it and turn to some other work.

Seventh days after Steve's first race at River Downs, he set a record at that track. He had brought in 120 winners during that time. On each of eight different days, he brought in four winners.

From River Downs, he moved on to Arlington Park and Hawthorne, near Chicago. Then, he went back to Churchill Downs in the Fall of 1976. In the first six months of his career, he won more than once in every four rides.

On November 30, Steve moved on to Aqueduct Race Track in New York. The weather was turning cold. To keep warm, Steve, now weighing 95 pounds and 5'1" tall, bundled up.

"It's so cold riding in New York," he said in December. "I have to wear gloves and earmuffs and sometimes wrap Saran Wrap around my feet to keep them warm. But I love to ride horses and I'm getting a chance."

The cold was not only uncom-

Winter racing means bundling up. Wide World Photos

fortable, but dangerous. A jockey thinks twice about driving between several horses when the wind is gusting. A sudden wind may blow his horse, or another, just enough off course to cause a terrible collision.

While he was racing at Aqueduct, Steve lived with Chuck Taliaferro, a trainer, at his home on Long Island. Often, he left for the track by six in the morning. He might have to see trainers, or exercise a few of their horses. After that came the full racing day.

The days were long for him. He had promised to keep up on his schoolwork. "One of the things my father and I agreed on was that I finish high school." Back in Walton, he had been making mostly A's and B's. To complete his studies, he was taking his courses by correspondence.

So, despite the tiring day, Steve did an hour or two of homework most days. By 9. p.m., he was usually off to bed. Sometimes, the 11 p.m. news would show Steve on TV. That was too late for him to watch. Steve was fast asleep by then.

The season at Aqueduct started badly. Steve lost his first four races. Then, he rode a 4-year-old named Illiterate, who hadn't won a race in almost eight months. Steve kept her close to the leaders. Then, with an eighth of a mile to go, he rammed her through an opening. Illiterate won by half a length.

In his next 51 rides at Aqueduct, Steve had seven winners—good, but not unusual. Then he got hot.

The racing season at Aqueduct ran 21 days. In that time Steve brought in 29 wins of the 141 horses he rode. That meant one of every five horses he raced was a winner.

On December 11, he brought in five winners in one day. One of the horses, Frampton Delight, had odds of 19-1 (one chance of 19 to win). In one six-day period, he brought in 23 winners. It broke the New York State record of 22 victories for the same period, set two years before.

Watching Steve, former jockey Sammy Renick said, "He has great hands.

When he brought "Rare Joel" in for a win at Aqueduct, he became the first jockey whose horses earned over $5 million in one year. Wide World Photos

Horses settle in and run kindly for him. Few jockeys have this touch. Steve hits the horse at the right time, which is a feel, a gift he has."

When Aqueduct closed for the Christmas holidays, Steve looked forward to going home. He had brought in 240 winning horses in the seven months he had been riding. His mounts had earned well over $1 million. Experts were predicting great things for him. At the rate he was going, they said, he could win 425 races in a full season. (No New York rider had won even 300 races in a year.) They said he might even bring in $6 million in 1977! (No jockey had ever brought in $5 million in winners.)

By December 23, 1976, Steve wasn't thinking too much about his future. What he wanted most was to get home for Christmas. He missed his parents and his brothers, Doug, 13, and Kerry, 7. 1977 was something he'd think about later—after the holidays.

Ping Pong is a good way to relax. Wide World
Photos

CHAPTER THREE

1977, A RECORD-BREAKING YEAR

Steve started 1977 by going to California's Santa Anita Race Track. Ronald McAnally, a trainer for the horse Pocket Park, asked for him. "I only knew what I had read about him. But we were strapped for a rider and I put the call in to Steve after I had talked to our manager in the East about him."

McAnally added, "He's been riding in the East when most of the top riders have been out here. He's young and doesn't have a weight problem. He can cope with the cold back there by wearing more clothes than most of the other riders. It all adds up. It's part of the reason he's

winning, why he can come out here and get mounts that other apprentices can't."

On his first of six Sundays at Santa Anita, Steve rode Pocket Park to second place in an important race. The lead horse bumped him. Steve didn't try to jerk his horse out of the trouble. He just let him settle back into his gait again. Because of that, Pocket Park came on again. He would have caught and passed the horse that bumped him if the race had gone on a bit longer. As it turned out, the lead horse was "fouled" and Steve, though he came in second, won the race.

His work schedule was killing. During the week he was racing at New York's Aqueduct track. After a full day of racing on Saturdays, he rushed to the airport. There he took a 6 p.m. flight to Los Angeles. Sunday afternoon, he was racing at Santa Anita. Then, Sunday evening, he was again at the airport for a late flight

Steve with Ronald McAnally, trainer of "Pocket Park." Los Angeles Turf Club, Inc. - Santa Anita Park

back to New York. The late flight is called "the red eye special," because you don't get much sleep. It got Steve into New York about six hours before his first race at Aqueduct on Mondays.

During the racing week of January 10, he rode 51 horses between Monday and Saturday. He took 23 of them to the Winner's Circle. Three of the days he had five winners each. No jockey ever had such a week.

Only six weeks after the '77 season started, Steve had become the first jockey ever to pass the $1 million mark in winnings so early in the year. At Aqueduct, by February 11, he brought in 87 winners in 279 rides.

In the following months, Steve went on making records. By early May, he was averaging wins on about 30% of his mounts, which is almost unheard of in horse racing. A 15% winning average is considered great.

On the way to the track aboard "Pocket Park."
Los Angeles Turf Club, Inc. - Santa Anita Park

In the Winner's Circle again. Los Angeles Turf Club, Inc. - Santa Anita Park

Then, on May 23, Steve had a bad fall. He was riding Bay Streak in the fourth race at Belmont Park, N.Y. Suddenly, the horse's foreleg snapped. Bay Streak went down. Steve hit the ground, blacking out. Three horses piled up. Jockey Jorge Velasquez, on one of the three, also fell. Velasquez' left foot was fractured at the ankle and heel. But Steve suffered even worse injuries. He broke the ulna bone in his right arm just above the wrist. He fractured the middle bones on two fingers and one rib, all on the right side. It took 10 stitches to close a cut above his right eye, and he had a slight concussion.

Both Steve's horse and Velasquez' had to be destroyed because of their injuries.

When Steve left the hospital, his doctor said it would take six weeks for complete healing of his arm fracture. But Steve had the cast removed after two weeks. He began doing yoga exercises and lifting weights. He strengthened himself to the point that he wouldn't stay away from

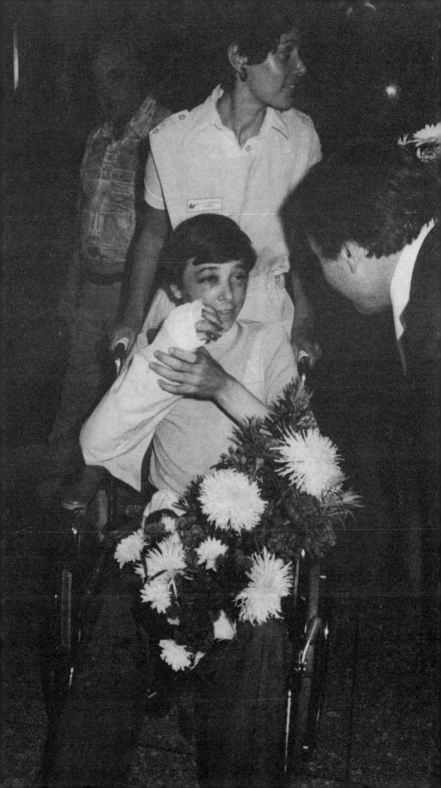

the track any longer. That was a good sign. The famous jockey Eddie Arcaro once said, "You're not a real jockey until you've broken a collarbone, five times." Some riders, after a bad fall, lose their nerve. Not Steve. He couldn't wait to get back. Thirty-one days after the accident, he was racing again.

On his very first day back, he rode a horse called Little Miracle. He drove through the other horses in the stretch and brought Little Miracle in first. Reporters and photographers mobbed him. In his quiet way, Steve explained his win. "Patience," he said. "It's a virtue."

Steve rode 16 races the first three days back. He won five and finished in the money on six others. That week he passed the $3 million mark in winnings. It was an amount no apprentice had ever won in one season. Only 11 full-fledged jockeys have made that much *in a year*. Steve had done it in only five months!

Steve holds up his broken wrist after release from the hospital. Wide World Photos

*First day back after his accident, Steve rode "Lit-
tle Miracle" to a win.* **Wide World Photos**

Steve stands on scale the last day as an apprentice, with Bill Shoemaker looking on. Wide World Photos

On June 27, one year after his fifth win, Steve lost his apprentice status. Some experts felt the loss of his five-pound weight advantage would make a difference in his performance. It didn't.

The rest of the year was a repeat of what went before. It seemed "Stevie Wonder" could do no wrong. Race goers screamed his praises. Experts clucked their tongues in amazement. The little kid from Kentucky with the pale face and the big, serious brown eyes broke record after record.

In 1977, Steve won 434 races at major New York tracks. He broke the record of 299 set by Jorge Velasquez in 1976.

He became the youngest jockey to lead the money list. Most of his wins were for small sums. Then, on September 10, Steve won his first really big money (over $100,000) on Affirmed. He followed that with another big-money win on the same horse in October. But even before that win, he had passed the earning record of

Here Steve shows programs with races he won circled. He set a record of twice having six wins in one day. Wide World Photos

Angel Cordero, Jr., set in 1976, of nearly $5 million.

In early December, riding a three-year old filly named Little Happiness, Steve brought his win money to over $6 million. That same day he took second place in another race, adding another $2,640 to his astonishing record. "It's nice," was what he said at the end of that day.

"You always want to win, sure," Steve says. "But the important thing is to get the most out of your horse. If he runs the best he can, wherever he finishes, I feel good—for him and for me. And when you cross that finish line first on a horse who is not the best, and you know it, that's the greatest feeling of all."

By the end of 1977, Steve was considered the leading jockey for 1977 in North America. The honor was based on races won (482) and money won ($6,087,800). He was only the second jockey in 18 years to head both lists in the same year. He was the youngest to top the money-won list.

Steve's remarkable talent and sportsmanship earned him three of racing's highest honors—the Eclipse Awards: as Apprentice Jockey, as Journeyman Jockey, and the Eclipse Award of Merit. The Award of Merit was given for "his inestimable and far-reaching contributions to the sport of thoroughbred horse racing."

To cap a fantastic year, *Sports Illustrated* Magazine named him "Sportsman of the Year" for 1977.

It takes a great horse and a great jockey to make a winning combination. What makes a great horse—a "thoroughbred?"

Steve, assisted by former jockey Louis Olah, selects his silks for the 104th running of the Kentucky Derby. **Wide World Photos**

40

CHAPTER FOUR

WHAT MAKES A THOROUGHBRED?

What's a thoroughbred?

It's the world's fastest racehorse. It can run up to 45 miles an hour carrying over 100 pounds on its back.

It's a graceful, beautiful animal, with a will to win. It has spirit, "heart." Thoroughbreds have been known to struggle on to the finish line even after breaking a leg.

All thoroughbreds can be traced back to three horses imported into Europe in the 1700s. They were Arabian stallions, though they probably didn't come from Arabia. They probably came from Turkey, Armenia, and Mesopotamia. These stallions were mated with native English mares. The result was a horse that was fast, and combined the sturdy quality of the English horses with the beautiful and spirited quality of the Arabian.

The thoroughbred was created for one purpose—to run faster than any horse had ever run before. England had been a nation of horse racers from the time of the Romans. By the 1600s, racing had become a national passion. Fortunes were bet on the outcome of a single race. Almost every rich man owned a racing stable. The man who could breed the fastest horses could win the most races. And the most money.

The three horses credited with being the ancestors of all today's thoroughbreds are the Byerly Turk, the Darley Arabian, and the Godolphin Barb.

Typical of how each of these horses arrived in England is the story of the Godolphin. It is said that the horse

The thoroughbred "Khaled". California Thoroughbred Breeders' Association

Weanlings—*foals just weaned from their moth-ers*. California Breeders' Association

was foaled in Arabia about 1724 in a rich prince's stable. He was called Scham, which means "the chief." When he was a two-year-old, he was sent as a gift to the king of France.

After the long voyage, the stallion was in poor condition. Also, the king did not like his small size and fiery temper. So, Scham was soon sold to a poor Frenchman. The man set the stallion to pulling a water wagon through the streets of Paris. He didn't get on with the horse. He fed him poorly, and beat him often. One day, a Quaker from England saw the horse being flogged, and he could not stand the unkindness. He bought the horse, and took him to England.

In England, Scham became the property of a London coffeehouse owner. Then, he was sold to a Lord Godolphin who had a racing and breeding stable.

In Lord Godolphin's stable was a mare named Roxanna. He wanted to mate Roxanna with a fine stallion named Hobgoblin. Fearing the mare might kick Hobgoblin, he put Scham in with her. If

Roxanna was going to kick, let it be this lesser horse who got hurt.

However, Roxanna accepted Scham, and refused to mate with the finer stallion. The result of their mating was a foal named Lath. He was one of the fastest horses in England. He and his offspring were the first of the Godolphin Barb's line of thoroughbreds.

A race horse weighs from 1,000 to 1,400 pounds. It is about 16-17 hands high, from the ground to the highest point of the withers, or ridge between the shoulder bones. (A hand is four inches. 16 hands equal 64 inches.)

The horse's front legs carry most of its weight and act as shock absorbers. The front legs are the ones most often broken. When a horse breaks its leg, it is usually destroyed because nothing can be done to help it.

Horses can see forward, sideways, and a little behind, but not above. Their oval eyes are set on the sides of their heads. This is why horses frighten easily. One eye sees an object before the other

Thoroughbred mare and her eight hour old foal.
California Breeders' Association

does. Blinders (leather flaps) are often attached to a horse's bridle to prevent side vision.

Horses have sharp hearing. A jockey can tell what his horse is about to do by watching the ears. If they shoot forward, the horse has heard or seen something that may frighten it. If the ears go flat against the head, it is angry.

The mare carries her foal for about 11 months before giving birth. The time varies from 10 to 14 months. The baby can stand and run within an hour after birth. A horse is born without teeth. By the time it is a year old, it has six pairs of upper and lower cutting teeth and is about half-grown. Most horses reach full height and weight at the age of five. At that age they have a full set of teeth. Males have 40, females, 36 teeth. Thoroughbreds reach full growth at the age of seven.

Horses usually live 25 to 30 years. Some have lived to 40 or more. One year of a horse's life equals about three of a man's. A seven year old horse, then, has aged equal to a 21-year-old human.

Mare and foal. California Breeders' Association

Horses have good memories. A colt, if frightened, won't forget what frightened it. Years later it will react with fear at the same thing. Horses are timid and easily frightened. They have strong likes and dislikes, especially toward other horses. Training is usually done by rewarding good actions and punishing bad ones.

No matter when they are born, all race horses have the same official birthday, January 1. All become a year older on each New Year's day. This system is used to qualify the horses for races limited to certain ages. Only three-year-olds can race in the Kentucky Derby, for instance.

This, then, is the thoroughbred, the horse Steve Cauthen knows best. But what of the jockey? How does he become "great"?

A young thoroughbred. California Thoroughbred Breeders' Association

Steve received the Woodlawn Vase for winning the 103rd Preakness Stakes at Pimlico Race Track. Wide World Photos

CHAPTER FIVE

WHAT MAKES A GREAT JOCKEY?

Steve is a great race rider. What makes him so?

First of all, he is small—only 5'1". He weighs less than the 115-118 pound maximum allowed for a jockey. Though small, he is very strong. It takes great strength to control 1,000 pounds of pent-up energy, moving at nearly 45 miles an hour.

Steve has great courage. Riding race horses is very dangerous. More than

one jockey has died in racing spills. Broken bones, internal injuries, and fractured skulls are not uncommon. But as well as courage, he has intelligence. He is coolheaded. He can think and react quickly. When he sees a chance to slip into a narrow opening or move to the rail, he acts instantly.

He's able to understand and follow his trainer's instructions. No one knows the horse as well as the trainer. He can tell the jockey if the horse is lazy or willing, if he likes the lead, or does best by coming up from behind.

Steve has a good sense of balance. He can move smoothly with the horse's stride. He sits almost weightlessly over the horse. He loosens the reins in the start of the race to let the horse start easily. But then he knows how to tighten his hold on the horse smoothly. That way he gets the horse to move into an even stride.

Steve accepts the "Big Sport of Turfdom" Award in Miami, Florida. Wide World Photos

Steve has good hands. Willie Shoemaker, who has won over 7,000 races, believes that "the secret is in the reins. In the end, it's between the rider's hands and the horse's mouth." The hands control the reins. The reins are attached to the metal bit in the horse's mouth.

His father, Tex, says, "It's the feet and the hands and the head" that matter. "That's the balance. You have to be able to think. They all go together."

Steve says, "I like horses to pick up the bit. When they wanna run, they run, y'know? You gotta try to get them to pick the bit up and do their own thing."

Shoemaker describes Steve this way: "He sits nicely without a lot of lost motion. But there's something else too. And that's hard to explain. Horses run better for some riders than for others. I believe that. And Cauthen's horses seem to

Typical of Steve's riding style is this shot with his face almost buried in the horses mane. Los Angeles Turf Club, Inc. - Santa Anita Park

Leaving the Starting Gate. Los Angeles Turf Club, Inc. - Santa Anita Park

run well no matter what their pattern is. He has everything it takes."

Kenny Church, former rider, says, "You never see him overwhip or yank on his horse. They run for him because he doesn't abuse them."

Still, a jockey is only as good as the mount he's riding. Most experts say that 90% of the win depends on the horse. The jockey may count for only 1 to 10% of the effort. A terrific jockey can't bring in a win on a slow horse. Most horses have to be coaxed to do their best. That's where a jockey's ability is important.

The "thinking" race rider has to keep an eye on the other horses all the time. How good is the horse that the jockey in the lead has under him? Where are the other horses? If he turns his mount loose at a certain point, where will the others be? What will they be doing?

There are lots of ways to lose a race. A jockey can let his horse run too fast, too soon. In the last moments, the horse has nothing left to give. The jockey can wait too long and get blocked. He can get pushed too far out on the track or get pinched in too tight along the rail. He can fight his horse too much, trying to hold him back. The horse may get angry and spit out the bit. The jockey can pace badly, drop the whip, lose his stirrups, fall.

But the making of a great jockey is even more than correcting these faults. To get where he is, Steve needed to ride good mounts. That's where selecting a good agent was important.

An agent works for a jockey by selecting horses for him to ride with good chances of winning. Then, he must talk the horse's trainer into using the jockey. For this work, the agent receives 25% of the jockey's earnings. An agent may only work for one apprentice jockey and one full-fledged jockey at the same time.

Lenny Goodman became Steve's agent in 1976. During the summer of that year, Steve went to Saratoga, New York, to race. While there, his father talked to Goodman about becoming Steve's agent. Goodman had handled some of the finest riders. He hadn't taken on an apprentice in 25 years.

"I saw Steve ride in two races at Saratoga," Goodman says. "He finished next to last in both, on horses that didn't have a chance. But the talent was there. He wasn't afraid. He knew how to wait. He could switch the whip. He had balance. A feeling comes over you when you see one like him. So few have what he has."

Lenny Goodman and Steve are from very different backgrounds. Mr. Goodman is about 55. He's a street-wise New Yorker who smokes cigars. In contrast, Steve is a farm boy. He chews gum. He doesn't smoke, drink, or go to dances much. His interests are simple. Enough to eat, a few clothes, gas for the car. (Steve drives a 1977 Cougar, a gift from River Downs Race Track in Ohio.)

As soon as Lenny Goodman took over as agent, he began lining up solid horses for Steve to ride. Steve was still a "bug boy." Most trainers don't like to use "bugs." But, if the apprentice can really ride, that's different. Then, the weight advantage of five pounds may make the horse run even better. So, the bug boy may get to ride some of the best horses. Steve's riding ability, his agent, and the fact that he could ride five pounds lighter than others gave him an edge.

As his fame spread, newsmen began calling him "Stevie Wonder." Fan letters began arriving, six or seven a day, mostly from girls. They wanted his picture. "The ones that wrote saying I'm the greatest and all that junk, I throw away," Steve said. Along the way, he made a record, "And Steve Cauthen Sings, Too." Quite a lot to take in for a kid so young.

Steve has all the qualities it takes to be a great athlete, a great race rider. But he has something else, too. "He's patient and he's a hard worker. He's also quiet and humble about his ways. He's well liked. People are willing to help him," jockey Darrel McHargue says.

Steve enjoys his success, but doesn't allow it to change him. All he wants is to do his best. "If the money

Steve talks to fans as he promotes his country-western record called "And Steve Cauthen Sings, Too." Wide World Photos

comes, it's great. But it's not the only thing
I think about. I just want to be happy," he
says.

CHAPTER SIX

A DAY IN THE LIFE OF STEVE CAUTHEN

The alarm rings at 6:30 a.m. for Steve. Maybe he's in a motel room. Maybe he's in a bedroom of a friend's home in the city where he will be racing. Steve wakes quickly, washes, dresses, and, without breakfast, heads out to the track in his '77 Cougar.

Picture the track. In February, it is Santa Anita in California. The stands are empty, waiting for the crowds which will arrive by 1 p.m. for the day's races. Now, at 7:15 a.m., maybe 30 people mull around the snack bar at track level. Some warm their hands around the hot coffee cups they hold. Trainers are here, and owners, and the curious.

It's cold now. In the distance the mountains loom sharply, like cardboard cutouts, against the blue sky. In the foreground are palm trees, the oval track, an inner track of turf, and still another inner circle where special parties can be held.

It's 7:30. From the barns come the exercise men and women. There are 1,700 horses stabled at Santa Anita, with 500 more held at nearby tracks. All must be exercised regularly.

As famous horses gallop by the stands, an announcer broadcasts who they are. Some of the horses wear bandages on their legs. It increases heat in the leg, which increases circulation. Some of the horses wear blinkers to keep their attention straight ahead. Many of the workers have been up since 4 a.m. That's when the

Santa Anita Race Track during racing season.
Los Angeles Turf Club, Inc. - Santa Anita Park

grooms arrive to clean out the stables, feed the horses and brush them down.

Steve parks in his marked space in the parking lot. He wears tan pants and a brown jacket. He buys a cup of coffee at the snack bar and joins Lenny Goodman and Laz Barrera, a trainer. They talk about the horses Steve will ride that day. Steve may be asked to take out one or another horse so he can become familiar with it. He says he can get the feel of a horse in five minutes.

Morning workouts are over by 9 a.m. Now Steve goes home and changes clothes. Then he comes back to the jockey's room at the track and eats breakfast. He only eats twice a day. "I don't need to watch my diet for weight, because I'm light. But I'm careful about what I eat. I try to develop good eating habits." He likes most foods, but especially seafood —shrimp, lobster, and other fish.

Long before the races begin, grooms are at work feeding, and grooming the thoroughbreds in the barns at the track. Los Angeles Turf Club, Inc. - Santa Anita Park

Afternoons, he will be working. There are nine races each afternoon. The race takes only a minute or two. But there is a half hour between each. That gives spectators a chance to view the next race's horses in the paddock, before they go out to the field. It also gives them time to place bets.

Before each race, a valet sets out Steve's gear. His boots will be shined. His "silks," the brightly colored shirt and cap, worn with white pants, will be selected. The colors stand for the owner's horse. Steve may trim his whip, knowing the whip is an extension of his hands. He wears goggles, which protect his eyes from the dirt and mud that fly during the race. As one pair of goggles get muddy, he pushes them down. Beneath is another, clean pair.

The stands where the spectators sit face a large oval track. Before each

Steve getting groomed before the Aqueduct race that boosted his purse over the $6 million mark. Wide World Photos

race, machines rake the rich brown soil of the mile-long track making it smooth again. If it is very dry, water wagons send out a spray to hold down the dust. The starting gate rolls onto the track. Soon it will be time for the race to begin.

A bugle sounds the "call to post." Now the thoroughbreds enter the track from the paddock area and parade past the stands. A jockey sits on each horse. Each jockey rides his horse past the stands, then to the starting gate stalls. Position is decided by drawing numbers early in the day. When all the horses are in their stalls, the starter presses a button. The gates swing open and a bell rings. The announcer shouts, "They're off!"

When Steve wins, he brings his mount to the winner's circle in front of the stands. There he is photographed with his horse. After each race, he and all the other jockeys are weighed, holding their saddles.

Racing on a muddy track makes for muddy faces.
Los Angeles Turf Club, Inc. - Santa Anita Park

About 6 p.m., he goes back to his motel. He will either dine out with trainers, owners, or friends, or cook for himself. He says he can't cook well—only eggs and hamburgers—so he mostly eats out.

Evenings, when he gets back from dinner, he may do homework. He has about six hours of work a week and will graduate in 1978. He's in bed by 9:30 or 10 p.m.

Does he get lonesome for close friends and family? "I miss my brothers," he said. "But I'm a big boy now and I've been away for almost two years. I miss my family very much because I love them. But you get used to it. You realize how much you miss them most when you get to see them, then have to leave to go back to work. But I enjoy what I do, my work. It keeps me happy, and busy." He goes home about twice a year to visit. His parents visit maybe a week at a time, a few times a year. "We talk a lot on the phone."

Steve's friends are nearly all older people connected with racing. "I enjoy

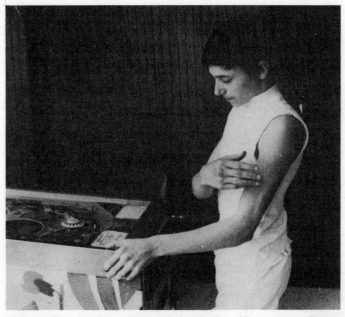

*When Steve Cauthen visited the Keystone Race
Track to ride in the Prestige Heritage Stakes he
passed the time playing pin ball.* Wide World
Photos

Steve tries to keep a poker face while playing cards before racing at Belmont Park. Wide World Photos

older people. I like to learn from them. They're interesting." When he goes home, his school friends treat him as they always did. He gets along well with the jockeys he works with. Sometimes they do things together, maybe go to dinner.

Steve works five days a week, sometimes six. He's usually off Mondays and Tuesdays when the track is closed. On days off he likes to sleep, watch TV, bowl, go to movies, play cards, ping pong, or tennis. He's pretty good at tennis. He's trying to learn to dance. Sometimes he goes to discos with friends. He doesn't have a special girl friend.

Most of Steve's reading is about horses. He likes stories in the racing newspaper and articles in horse magazines.

He doesn't like hard rock, nor does he play a musical instrument. The music he does enjoy comes from the radio. He likes sounds with a good beat, with lyrics, pleasant music.

When he was asked who his heroes were, Steve said, "I admire different people in different sports. I admire excellence in any field. I've met a lot of great people from different fields. The truly great ones are truly nice people."

He doesn't like being pushed by the press. "When you get a little success, people want to know about you. It's very nice, but it's trying. You have so very little spare time, and giving interviews takes that much more time from you. You're always in front of people. I like to be alone some of the time to relax and think about things. About life. About how things are going."

Steve says he'll ride as long as he can. "Willie Shoemaker is small. He can ride as long as he's able." But Steve may grow. "You never know in this business. You have to want to be on top. You must always strive for excellence. Keep pushing to learn new things and be better. I get tired very much of pushing. But I like to ride, and I want to be on top."

What does he think about when he races? "I've been at the gate [starting gate] maybe 3,000 times this past year. You don't get nervous. You're thinking

Much of Steve's reading is about horses or racing.
Wide World Photos

about the race and where you want to be. And you try to break accordingly. You want to go to the lead."

Sometimes he talks to the horse, but not often. "You yell at him a little if he's a young horse and isn't paying attention. Sometimes you talk in a soothing tone to calm the horse down." Steve says he can "feel" the horse through his hands. The horse gains confidence in you, through your hands. "I love horses. They are not dumb animals. They're very intelligent."

The biggest thrills for Steve come with winning big races. Or six races in a day. Or, if he beats someone in a photo finish. "Whenever you do something near perfection, that's a good feeling."

Although racing is rather dangerous, Steve says the more you ride, the more you gain confidence. When you are good enough to control the horse, there's nothing to be afraid of.

Steve with Willie "The Shoe" Shoemaker. Los Angeles Turf Club, Inc. - Santa Anita Park

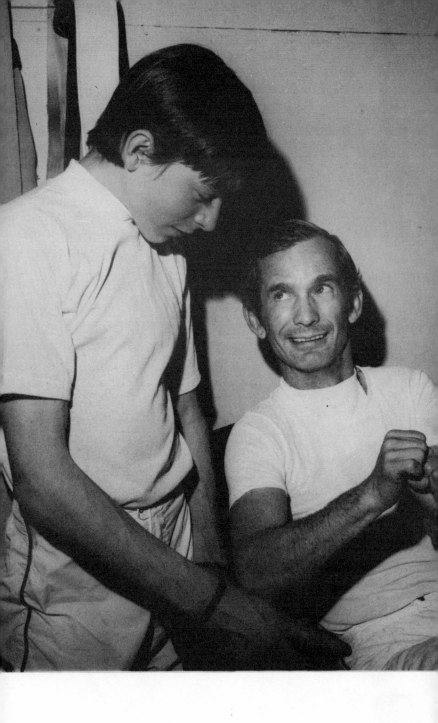

Here is "Seattle Slew" with jockey Jean Cruguet, winners of the 1977 Triple Crown. Wide World Photos

CHAPTER SEVEN

TRIPLE CROWN

Steve turned 18 on May 1, 1978. Ahead laid the greatest challenge of all—the chance to win the Triple Crown. The most important of racing honors, the Crown has been awarded to only 7 jockeys in history. To earn it, the rider must win 3 special events in a single year—the Kentucky Derby, The Preakness and The Belmont Stakes. These races are held two weeks apart and only 3 year old race horses may compete.

Racing across the finish line to win the 104th running of the Kentucky Derby is Steve Cauthen on "Affirmed." Wide World Photos

On May 6, Steve entered the first of the three events—The Kentucky Derby. Riding Affirmed, a colt he had taken to victory in many other races, he was not favored to win. Alydar, jockeyed by Jorge Velasquez, was the favorite.

However, Steve believed in his gleaming orange ball of fire. He said Affirmed was the most intelligent horse he'd ever ridden, with the heart of a thoroughbred.

There was only one worry. Once Affirmed took the lead, he tended to relax. Knowing this, Steve let his mount stay in 3rd place until halfway into the mile and a quarter race. Then, he let out the stops.

In the last seconds, Alydar came up fast from behind. But it was too late. Steve and Affirmed crossed the finish line a length and a half ahead of their rivals.

Two weeks later, the same pair—horse and man—were in Baltimore for the Preakness. Again, the contest was between Affirmed and Alydar. This time, though, Velasquez brought Alydar up sooner. As they headed for home, Alydar came

At Pimlico Race Track in Baltimore, Md., Steve once again rides "Affirmed" to victory, winning the Preakness Stakes. Wide World Photos

within a neck of Affirmed, then inched closer. But Affirmed wouldn't let *any* horse take the lead. He crossed the finish line first, a nose ahead of Alydar.

With two down and one yet to go, the excitement grew. Could Steve do it once more? If so, he would be the youngest jockey ever to win the Triple Crown.

The answer came on Saturday, June 10th, 1978, at Belmont Park. Again, the battle narrowed to the two A's, Affirmed and Alydar, though three other horses also ran. It was the longest of the three races. Alydar was considered the stronger horse, so the distance might be in his favor.

Steve didn't push Affirmed at first. He wanted to save his colt's energy for that final stretch of the long race. About halfway into the mile and a half race, Alydar moved up. Running 6 lengths ahead of the other horses, the two great thoroughbreds raced side by side, stride for stride, head to head.

Steve was squeezed against the rail on the left. Alydar crowded him on the

Steve Cauthen and "Affirmed" are led to the Winner's Circle after winning the 1978 Triple Crown! Wide World Photos

right. It was so tight, he could hardly use his whip. In the final moment, he switched the whip to his left hand. He had never hit Affirmed on that side before. The courageous colt got the message. He gave Steve just a little bit more, running as he never had before.

Coming across the finish line, Steve threw up his left hand in triumph. Affirmed had just won the 11th Triple Crown by a head.

What now? At 18, Steve Cauthen seems to have everything. Money. Fame. The joy of achieving his greatest dreams. He will stay in racing as long as he remains small, does well, and enjoys it. After that, he may go back to school to become a vet. Meanwhile, winning the Triple Crown is, in Steve's words, "Somethin' else!" Steve, the Kid, the wonder boy of racing—is something else too.

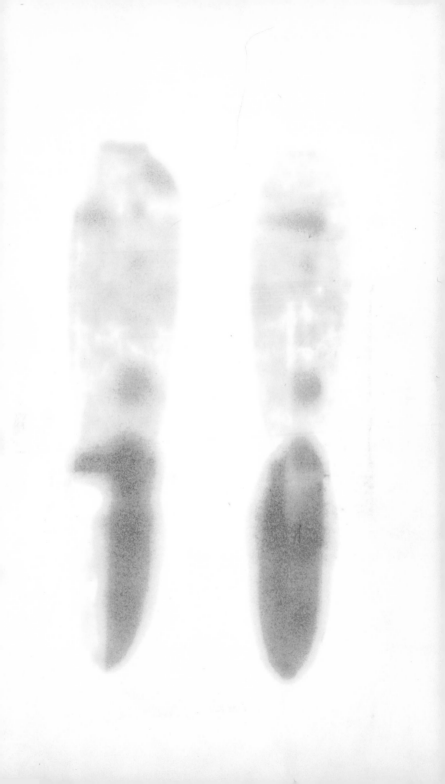